Spark Your Inner Warrior: Reignite Your Body, Mind & Spirit

By

Nathan Sparks

Dedication

I want to thank my lovely wife for putting up with me throughout this project. I love you more than I can express with words on this page. Every day I am truly amazed that I get to see your incredible smile and spend my life with the love you give.

To the rest of my family, thank you for your love, support and time. Your guidance for this book has made it the masterpiece it is today.

To Tori, thank you for being my editor in chief and providing your scholarly knowledge, as it was invaluable for the success of this book.

Table of Contents

Disclosure

Spark Your Inner Warrior: Reignite Your Body, Mind & Spirit is not intended as a substitute for professional medical advice. Additionally, you should rely only on your doctor or another qualified health professional health for personal advice regarding a medical condition or your health.

Spark Your Inner Warrior: Reignite Your Body, Mind & Spirit

Nathan Sparks

Introduction

"A major contributor to the genesis of many diseases... is an overload of stress induced by unconscious beliefs. If we would heal, it is essential to begin the painfully incremental task of reversing the biology of belief we adopted very early in life. Whatever external treatment is administered, the healing agent lies within. The internal milieu must be changed. To find health, and to know it fully, necessitates a quest, a journey to the center of our own biology of belief. That means rethinking and recognizing—re-cognizing: literally, to "know again"—our lives."

— Gabor Maté, When the Body Says No: The Cost of Hidden Stress

According to Buddha, we're all born anew every morning, which is why what we do each day matters. Thinking along those lines will reveal an important life-truth to you: we're more than just our bodies. It follows that to lead balanced lives and perform better, we must ensure our physical, emotional, mental, and spiritual selves align.

It might surprise you that your body affects your mental and emotional states. But it'd totally knock off your socks to learn that it also influences your spirit. Additionally, the reverse is true! All our selves are interconnected, which is why treating them separately doesn't work so well. A healthy body is in sync with a healthy mind and spirit and vice versa.

However, let's not jump the gun and start you off with an introduction to each aspect of our self:

The Three Yous

Your Spirit

You may be a believer of one of the multitudes of faiths found in the world today. In that case, you probably view your spirit as the thread linking to you the Supreme Deity you follow. Or, like us, you may be more in touch with your inner self. In that case, you'd view your spirit as the essence of who you are. In either case, the spirit is the aspect of your three selves that assigns value, meaning, and purpose to everything else.

The spirit makes you more than a body responding to relentless pressures and excessive demands. It is the fertile field on which your well-being and optimal health will take root. If it is akin to barren land, then you'd find it hard to sustain both.

Your Mind

This is an aspect that most people are more familiar with since the mind is a powerhouse. It's like a magician who has stepped out in the arena and can perform miracles and feats of wonders. However, you may not be using yours that right. Ha! By that, we refer to running it on the fuel of spiritual significance.

Our thoughts have powered life on earth, making it extremely human-friendly. They gave us airplanes, and they imagined slushies. In short, they are our greatest assets that we can squander or channel. Should we ably channel their awesome energy in a clear direction and with an equally clear purpose, we can do so much more!

Your Body

If you expect your body to remain healthy, you'll need to start by meeting its core needs. It's a marvel that runs on more than ninety nutrients, which it picks from the food you eat. However, it will require other interventions that underpin our health. For example, meditation, massage, yoga, acupuncture, tai chi, and reflexology have great benefits.

Besides these, mastering the body's health cannot happen in the absence of water. Hydration is essential since nearly most physical diseases can be traced back to dehydration. Many infectious agents thrive in anaerobic conditions and in places where water is in short supply.

As evident, if you seek to transform all your three selves, you must respect their independent needs. Only by meeting those will you reach the state of interdependence on which our health relies.

Holistic Systems are Happy Systems

Heal One Self to Keep the Other Selves Healthy

It should be clear to you by now that all three of our selves are connected. Together, they form one holistic system. That's why we need to work on the ecology of all three. A healthy mind influences your body positively and enhances spiritual growth. The same is true about our physical health and spiritual well-being.

An escape from our mental world isn't possible. It's where our mind resides, as do all our experiences. However, your mind is comprised of two parts, subconscious and conscious. The subconscious mind is so much more powerful, making it worth our while to understand how it works. Our experiences – and the lessons we learn from them -- get dumped in the subconscious part of your brain. You may not even know it, but events from the past can still be affecting the way you act in the now. Therefore, if you transform the beliefs and attitudes you have, you can change things for your body and spirit.

It's best to come at optimum health from a place where your mind, body, and spirit are all aligned. A holistic approach that doesn't just focus on one part but addresses the whole person is the best for healing. It doesn't mean you should abandon traditional medicine. Not going to the doctor when you're running a fever won't help you – or the people who must put up with your irritable self! But conventional concepts of healing focus on treating illnesses from a physical perspective. That still leaves your mental and spiritual selves hanging.

Additionally, healing focused on a physical locus comes with a high risk of relapse. It's because it only seeks to treat one-third of your selves. So, we ask that you use traditional medicine in conjunction with a holistic approach. Doing so produces longer-lasting results.

The Connection between the Various Aspects

If one aspect of your self can influence the other two, it means the three remain in constant communication. So, when one of your selves is affected, information about it is instantly communicated to the rest of them. Hence, when you respond to that stimulus, you do so with your entire being.

Take fear as an example. When we're afraid, it prompts a response throughout our body. There's the effect that fear has on your mind, which makes you think panicked thoughts. Your emotions also begin to fluctuate wildly. On the other hand, your body also begins showing physical signs of fear. The usual indications are an increase in your breathing and heart rate, sweating, and a clenching in the stomach. At the spiritual end, you might begin praying for help or rescue. In other words, all aspects of our being would be experiencing the effects of fear.

That remains the same regardless of the emotion, situation, and other stimuli we experience. Pain, cravings, stress, trauma, joy, depression, illness, and excitement – we respond to them all with our entire being. This suggests a high level of interconnectedness between all three aspects. It's also why only approaches that seek to heal us physically, spiritually, and psychologically are the most successful ones.

You may have heard of how Buddhists train to reduce physical pain and discomfort by the actions of their minds. Chronic pain is nothing like the tiny aches that most of us carry around in our bodies. It's discomfort that's strongly influenced by how the brain processes the pain signals. That's why it can provoke strong emotional reactions, like fear, anxiety, and sometimes, even terror. What an individual will undergo depends on what they believe about those pain signals.

Even so, it is possible for Buddhists to manage their pain by engaging the selves other than the physical one. Deliberate relaxation in a reclining position for some time is one strategy people use. Once settled down, that person slows down their breathing. They can remain in this state or try visualization techniques for pain relief. For instance, they can transfer their focus from the source of the pain to another specific non-painful part of the body. Called altered focus, this method calls for the person to imagine the latter part altering in some way, such as by warming up or cooling down.

Therefore, the management of pain that our physical body is experiencing is possible through the manipulation of our mental and spiritual aspects.

Perception is Everything – What Health and Wellbeing Mean to You

Life flows like rivers do, which means it keeps changing as the conditions do. Like rivers will swell when it rains and recede during droughts, we also go through a constant series of adjustments. Just as a riverbank will transform with time, so do we. The bedrock responds to the changing seasons and the weather. Consequently, sometimes the river will flow smoothly while at other times, its flow will be impeded.

Likewise, we undergo all kinds of challenges on multiple fronts, i.e., physical, emotional, mental, and spiritual. As we experience them, we either adapt or resist in response. Whether we let these stressors keep us from growing or develop alongside them is up to us. In addition, the world around us doesn't remain the same either. Both our local and global environments are in flux. Trauma, disease, accidents, and death ensure that no two tomorrows are the same!

We aren't alone in this uniqueness. Life works like that for all humans. To remain healthy, we should find what works for our unique needs. Our fears and desires aren't the same. We're all combinations of differences in body types, cultures, genes, and personality. Our experiences, too, add more individuality to the mix. We make choices based on these characteristics, which have their own consequences. Some outcomes are long-term, while others are ephemeral. They can push our mind-body-spirit connection out of alignment in different ways. To understand how to regain that balance, we must first understand what health means to us individually.

What's It To Ya?

Say you meet the following two people. Which of the two would you consider healthy?

1. A 42-year-old individual has to stay at home due to a fever. They spend the day lying on the couch recuperating from the cold they caught and which has been going around at work. With little to no desire to eat, they can only rest until they feel well enough to return to their usual daily activities.

2. There's another 42-year-old who is chronically tired after having to work from an office desk for hours on end. When their energy begins to flag, they drink caffeinated energy drinks or munch on donuts. The consumption helps keep them awake and focused. To get to where they want to go, this individual hasn't taken any days off or vacations in months.

So, which of these feels healthier to you? Before you answer, consider this. What your response is going to be will depend on what health means to you. If to you, health is simply the absence of disease, then your vote would be for the second person. Sure, they don't have a fever and can still go to work. But might there not be something subtler and far-reaching affecting them?

This is why it's important to understand what we mean when we use a word (cue Princess Bride joke). After all, any term can have different meanings attached to it. Therefore, let's define what health and illness should mean to us:

Health represents a state where we are in a balance with our external and internal environments. Since it must respond to challenges from time to time – both chronic and acute—health is dynamic.

Illness or disease is its opposite, i.e., an imbalanced state where we must respond to challenges to regain the previous state of stability. Chronic illnesses overwhelm our resources, preventing us from responding.

Being healthy and well means that we can meet those challenges on all fronts—be they physical, spiritual, or mental. Even when temporarily ill, being in a state of balance ensures that we'll recover.

Now, let us look at those two individuals once more. Regardless of what your response would have been before, do you think the sick stay-at-home individual is less healthy than the one well enough to go to work? We hope that you don't. That's because a healthy person will adjust to an acute illness. They will go through the usual bodily responses and rise to the challenge. Fever is our body's way of letting us know that it's fighting off an infection. We should lend it a helping hand by doing nothing, i.e., resting.

On the other hand, the office-worker may look healthy. However, they aren't providing rest to their body as they should. Soon, the challenges in life will overwhelm the resources available to them. In conclusion, their approach to living is wholly unsustainable!

It's thus essential that we reform our perceptions of health and illness. Also necessary is for us to adjust how we live to meet both short- and long-term needs. Sustainable wellness is crucial. Do you think *you* have it?

Looking Within – An Exploration of Your Health

Now that we're using the same definitions for health and illness, it's time to find out how healthy you are. Below is a quiz that will help you explore where you stand right now in terms of health. Explore them and then revisit them some weeks later. It'll be interesting for you to see your point of view evolve and find a new point of focus.

Now, this exploration isn't about the scores since there's no one-size-fits-all way we can use to format these questions. So, don't worry about whether you're getting 100% of the answers right or wrong. Additionally, don't use this test to determine if you're experiencing optimal health or are at risk for disease. Instead, focus on how well you're connected with yourself and the quality of life. It's an opportunity for self-discovery and personal transformation. We'll discuss the practices that encourage well-being in the individual chapters later on.

Once you employ this section to figure out where you're now in terms of health, you can track your progress by comparing these results with the ones you get later on. Doing so will identify the areas that need further strengthening.

So, let's begin with the questions:

1. If we take wellness to be a state of being, would you say you were inhabiting it right now? Can you be healthy but not well or vice versa? Can you experience wellness even when your body is undergoing an illness?

2. What does wellness look like to me? Will I be able to recognize it in others? Do I see it in myself? If so, what does it feel like? Which senses am I using to determine wellness?

3. When I am not well, which part of the triad is most likely to be out of balance? Is my mind linked with the other aspects? Or, do I need to work on my spiritual self?

4. What's my daily schedule like? Are my practices impacting my health? How are they influencing my health? Which aspect are they working against the most?

5. Do I recognize my imbalances? Am I making a conscious effort to accommodate them? Or do I ignore the imbalances? Am I choosing the path of least resistance when I address them?

6. Since living requires making constant adjustments, do I make them in complete awareness?

7. Do I focus on my emotional health? Or, does all my attention go towards correcting physical health-based imbalances?

8. Can I partner up with someone when it comes to taking responsibility for our individual wellness and health? With whom would I partner? How would that work?

9. When was the last time I tried to change the way I live? Why did I make that decision? How did it go, and what did I learn from the experience? What's making me think of doing it again?

After figuring out exactly where you stand in terms of health and well-being, use the pointers below to create a wellness checklist. Try to go through it as often as you can, so you'll remain informed about yourself.

1. For the Hows, ask How am I…

    a) Eating?

    b) Sleeping?

    c) Exercising?

    d) Relaxing?

    e) Relating to the people around me, including loved ones?

    Then substitute Hows with Whys, Whens, and Wheres.

2. As you peruse this book, you'll discover different ways you can intervene and bring your health back on track. List those down on the wellness checklist. Your personal interventions will act as reminders and keep you on the path of regaining the mind-body-spirit balance.

    As an example, one of your personal interventions could be: I sleep well if I take the dog out for a walk after dinner. You'll find others in our Bite-Sized Personal Interventions sections – more on this below.

3. Finally, the most critical portion here. Just as you do with your wellness quiz, periodically reassess the answers you give to the questions on the wellness checklist.

Forging the Mind-Body-Spirit Connection

After perusing the previous section – or skimming it, come on, we all do it! – it might be clear to you that the synchronization of your three selves is crucial for health. Below, we mention several ideas that can help you forge a connection between that triad. While we'll go over other measures in much more detail later, we thought this would make a good starter pack.

Work out the Connection between Emotional Health and Physical Wellbeing

Thoughts and feelings make up our emotions. Often, we behave in a specific way because those emotions are at the helm. While calling your ex may or may not affect your health, emotions *can* influence your physical well-being! Since the three aspects are connected, your body responds to how you think or are feeling.

Not taking care of your emotional health can weaken your body's immune system. Don't buy it? Think back on all those times you were going through an emotional upheaval. Now, recall if your body was also fighting off a cold, flu, or other infections during such emotionally difficult times. Chances are, you were!

Is the reverse true? Would taking care of yourself physically also help you emotionally? It likely would. For instance, you can get relief from tension with exercise. Mind-body therapies have helped arthritis patients manage their pain. By incorporating brief periods of meditation into their daily schedule, those who regularly battle anxiety and depression can find a measure of peace and calm.

Dietary Concerns could be on Your Mind

Our food intake doesn't just affect our bodies; it can also do a number on our minds! When we overeat, we do so because of choosing a diet that isn't quenching our needs properly. Simple and fulfilling eating provides satiation and removes the need for dieting. Often, hunger is not our body's cry for food but an indication of dehydration. The next time you get the pangs, drink a glass of water. See if that does the trick before reaching for the crisps.

Serotonin, a neurotransmitter, controls our appetite and moods. It also regulates sleep and inhibits pain. Most of this chemical is produced in your GI tract. The gastrointestinal pipeline is studded with a hundred million nerve cells – neurons. That's just one way through which the food you eat isn't just affecting your body. It also guides your emotions!

Sleeping on the Job is Absolutely Necessary

It's essential that maintain a consistent sleeping pattern for your health. Among other things, regular sleep helps the body and mind maintain serotonin levels. Without it, our bodies become stressed. This stress can translate into various mental issues, such as depression, bipolar disorder, anxiety disorders, and ADHD. In short, sufficient sleep keeps both our bodies and minds in functioning order.

Spiritual Development, Physical Behavior, and Mental Health Go Hand in Hand

Our minds can help us sharpen essential survival skills, i.e., staying healthy and happy. Clearing out your daily schedule for a 30-minutes-long meditation period will hasten you on your journey of self-discovery. The rate of personal growth, too, can accelerate if we carve out that time for ourselves.

Make sure that you spend it in a peaceful spot and preferably amongst nature and fresh air. Walk barefoot on the grass or hug a tree to strengthen your connection to the earth and for spiritual enrichment. Watch a sunset with someone you love or play with your pet. This interval can calm you down and keep you from living in a permanent state of alarm. Therefore, when you change the environment your body's in, you also change your mind and bring peace to your spirit. The opposite is true as well. People who look after their spiritual well-being tend to lead better quality lives. Research on HIV/AIDs patients has shown that!

Gentler is Healthier on All Levels

Being gentle shows great strength. In addition, it also keeps you healthy! For one, an act of kindness can result in a *helper's high* due to the release of serotonin. Besides pumping the body full of the happy hormone, kindness also promotes psychological well-being by reducing anxiety levels. So, being gentle towards others is good for your mental health.

Kindness can also promote the release of the hormone, oxytocin. Known as a cardioprotective chemical, oxytocin also reduces inflammation. Thus, by being kind, you're protecting your body from illness!

Obviously, being gentle will also be great for personal growth and spiritual well-being.

Usage Instructions – How to Use this Guide

First off, let's understand that not everything in this book will work for everyone. As mentioned, we're too unique and unusual for that. However, we'd like to think most readers will find some practices and information in it useful. So, pick what works for you and implement it in your life.

In order to have a speedy and enjoyable healing journey, familiarize yourself with how this guide is structured. Besides this section introduces you to the importance of balance between your mind, body, and spirit, there are five other chapters. The first three will focus on the individual needs of the three aspects. At the end of each of these chapters, you'll find a section called 3 Bite-Sized Personal Interventions. Think of them as a snapshot of the information we cover in the chapters. What's more, these are ready-to-be-applied changes that you can practice daily.

There's also a chapter to help you view the individual needs of each aspect in the light of the other two. The last chapter informs readers where they can find further guidance on the mind-body-spirit connection and maintaining it.

So, are you ready? We knew you'd say that! Here we go…

Chapter 1 - Mind

The primary cause of unhappiness is never the situation but your thoughts about it. Be aware of the thoughts you are thinking. Separate them from the situation, which is always neutral, which always is as it is.

Eckhart Tolle

Mindset

The beliefs, attitudes, and assumptions conditioning how you see the world make up your mindset. It's how you will interpret what you see. However, you won't always be conscious of the components that make up your mindset.

Why the Right Mindset Matters

Your mindset has a significant and measurable effect on your well-being. It can make you resilient to stress and practice effective stress management – or it can do the opposite. It's plain to see that our mindset affects our health. As an example, this research on pain involved surgery patients. They were given morphine either via injection by a doctor or through automatic injections that came from a machine. The dosage of the drug was same for both the groups, but they weren't informed about when they'd be receiving it.

The researchers concluded that patients who had received doctor-injected morphine felt significantly more pain relief. Since the vehicle of the drug was the only real difference, results show that patient perception was the key here. If they thought another human being was caring for them, the patients showed heightened relief from pain.

While you might term the way the machine-injected patients reacted as a placebo response, that's not the case. Both groups got real injections and not placebos. So, what does that tell us about our mindset? That it definitely matters *and* influences our well-being.

Therefore, focusing on measures like eating well and regular exercising is good for your body. However, if you want to live more healthfully, you can't ignore the impact your mindset has on your well-being. It's also why a new field called psychoneuroimmunology has been developed. Students of psychoneuroimmunology look at how thoughts and feelings are connected to our disease resistance and health.

Mindset and Nutrition

If you haven't heard it before, it's time you did. Consuming a balanced and nutritious diet isn't the only thing that ensures you'll fare well. You aren't just what you eat but also what you think you're eating! One study that linked nutrition and mindset comes to us courtesy of the Stanford Mind and Body Lab. When served two milkshakes, the participants were conveyed two different messages. The first shake was light, sensible, and low-calorie. The second had almost five times as many calories, which made it an indulgent shake. What the participants were unaware of was that the calorific intake was the same for both shakes.

The researchers were interested in the self-reported levels of participants' levels of satiety vs. gherlin in their intravenous blood. Ghrelin is a hunger-promoting hormone that signals satiation when its concentration in the blood drops. Despite their calorific similarities, the participants displayed more satiation when they thought they had had the indulgent shake. The opposite was true for the other group.

Additionally, blood grehlin levels changed in both groups. The indulgent shake group showed a steep decline in hormone levels. Grehlin concentration remained the same for the other participants. In other words, what we believe we're eating determines our body's physiological response to food!

In another research on vegetable labeling and consumption, healthier foods tasted less appetizing to the participants. Such foods were also less satisfying and filling. The participants reached more often for the veggies when the foods were given indulgent and decadent names, such as sweet sizzlin' green beans. Anything that had light, low carbs, or an ordinary label was consumed the least. Thus, once again, the mindset played a huge role in the appraisal, consumption, and desirability of food.

An assessment of people over how they perceived chocolate cake also produced interesting results. Both participants – those who felt guilty when faced with cake and those who didn't – possessed similar eating intentions. However, the former group had lower self-control, which meant they were less likely to maintain their weight in the future. Here, too, the mindset controls the way those individuals acted.

In other words, mindset matters when it comes to what we eat, how much of it, and how our body responds physiologically. The takeaway from this section is that we should worry less about the caloric content and more about how delicious and stress-free the food that we're eating is. Paying more attention to the sensations food produces is more likely to leave us feeling satiated.

Mindset and Spirituality

Consider the number of times you've aimed to transform. However, you've given up as soon you encountered a difficult situation. The reason behind it is that spiritual transformation comes from a much deeper subconscious level. It cannot be rushed or faked!

Now we know mindset is linked to nutrition – and our physical bodies. Let's see in what ways is it also connected to our spirit:

1. No Such Thing as Linear Healing

When something opens up a wound or triggers you emotionally, see it as an opportunity. Use the occasion and elevate your spirit. Don't perceive it as a failure rather, take it as a chance to heal. Just like an onion, your spirit consists of many layers. Every time one of those layers is peeled back, work on healing what's been revealed. Each layer will require a specific time to get better. The process may even require revisiting the other healed-up layers that came before. Since linear healing isn't a thing, go with the flow.

2. Let Your Negative Emotions Come to the Front

Most of our pre-adult lives, we're taught that negative emotions are bad. We'll prefer to run, resist, or repress them – anything but deal with them. It's no wonder that's how we behave after being told to hush up whenever we cried. Expressing anger is considered a bad thing, and the people around you will immediately try calming you down.

What's the downside in all of that? Repressed emotions transform into anxiety and depression. Both are anathema to our mental health and well-being. After a lifetime's worth of training to suppress them, just try to push up against these emotions. You'll face strong resistance! So, what do you do with these *bad* feelings?

How about using them as teachers? Anger can fuel your creativity, while struggles with adversity often leave us open to new perspectives. Shame can make you more compassionate, and pessimism ushers in productivity. And those are just some of the so-called negative emotions!

3. Use Your Words

When we open our mouths, we're getting ready to create a whole emotional state. Likewise, by saying what we're thinking, we're choosing to affirm what's in our minds. Thus, our thoughts and emotions can influence what we go through in our lives. So, we should be mindful of what we speak, how we say it, and who we say it to – including ourselves.

The Road to the Right Mindset

So, we're on the same page when it comes to our mindset and life improvement. That's good! The next step we need to take is to carve our own paths leading to the right mindset. Here are several ideas that can help remove the roadblocks you might encounter:

1. *Walk Down Your Own Path*

The struggle with the concept of self-love is real! Almost every day, we learn a new example of how our lives should be. In the process, we end up comparing our life with that of others. That's never a good thing! Sure, you shouldn't stop striving to be better, healthier, or happier. However, do it in your own way and for only yourself – and nobody else.

If you were born unlike the others, there's a reason for that uniqueness. Why would you try to walk down a path that isn't meant for you? To be someone else? In short, what *you* consider to be success should be what matters the most. Don't focus on how others define it. To borrow the cheesiest of lines, be the best version of yourself.

2. *Eat Healthy and Unprocessed Food*

Sure, you may be thinking, we're just piling on the cliches now. However, that isn't our intention at all. We're underlining the importance of minimizing highly processed foods from your life. Mostly because they don't carry many nutritional benefits. In a way, by consuming them, you're doing your body an injustice.

Replace them with good nutrition. Choose foods that will let your body work at its absolute best. Try them, and you'll end up feeling really good. Such foods don't come with the nasty additives found in the other type. The first three you should dial back are caffeine, refined sugars, and excessive salt.

3. Find Your Tribe and Surround Yourself with Them

Those with an outlook that's positive and matches yours will give you a greater sense of well-being. So, connect with them and try new things with your friends. Spending time with such people will make you feel appreciated and loved. You'll laugh together, which can be a mood booster.

Moreover, when you surround yourself with a tribe like that, you'll also find the encouragement you need to strive towards your goals and be the best you!

4. Celebrate Everything!

Balancing the demands from the various areas in our lives makes things so hectic. We must meet them all, whether it's work, family, or friends. What this does is overwhelm us to the point that we forget what's really important.

For instance, having time that's just for you is essential for your well-being. Once you set aside such a slot, spend it doing what makes you happy. If all you want is to make an amazing cup of tea and then consume it in peace, DO IT! Or, your idea of Me Time might involve listening to music you love, then go ahead. DO IT! While you're doing whatever you find most suitable, pause for a minute. Appreciate that you have time that you can spend on yourself. Then continue DOING IT! Make this into a weekly thing.

5. Find a Hobby

Developing hobbies and skills can bring us joy. They can also bring a sense of purpose to our lives. Spending every waking hour while working or studying can make you feel underwhelmed with life. Keep your mindset positive by doing things that make you happy.

Now, your hobby can be anything that calls to you. Don't think, just jump in and start cultivating it – no matter how strange the territory where your interests lie! In addition, what attracts you may change from year to year. Follow the variation and always have something to look forward to!

6. Give Back to Get Some Back

Maintaining healthy relationships helps us maintain a positive mindset. One way we can do that is by becoming a part of a community. That involves reaching out and offering our support. For instance, do something nice for people you care about but have lost touch with. Or, call your grandmother if you haven't talked to her in a while. You can also volunteer and perform small acts of kindness.

Doing something positive without expecting something in return makes us feel good about ourselves.

7. Don't Stop...Talking!

Just like you shouldn't be burying your negative emotions, you shouldn't worry about talking about your feelings either. Whether you're feeling sad, disappointed, or angry, talk about it. Many of us think we'll be bothering others with our issues if we did that. However, it's talking that helps you process those feelings. Unless you do so, moving on from them will be very difficult.

Did that not convince you of the importance of letting things out? There's another way to express what you may be feeling. Start a journal – weekly if you don't have time for a daily jot-down session. Express yourself through entries, and you'll feel much better.

Cognition

The processes our mind uses to gain knowledge and understand things are known as cognition or cognitive processes. However, they aren't limited to just knowing and comprehension. Thinking, judging, recalling, and problem-solving are all the results of cognitive processes.□ These higher-level functions make it possible for us to learn languages, visualize, perceive things, and plan.

What It Is

Such processes affect our daily lives and even our health and well-being in the following ways:

1. Perceiving the World

Our body is bombarded with so many kinds of sensations in just minutes. However, the information gained via our senses requires processing. It's transformed into signals that our brain can interpret. The whole process from accepting the incoming data and its conversion into signals forms the perceptual process. Judging if the coffee cup is hot is as much the result of the cognitive processes as calculating a rocket's trajectory. □

2. *Finding the Meaning*

Forming impressions out of the endless amount of sensory experiences that the world throws at us is also a cognitive process. For this to happen, your brain records everything you experience. Later, it reduces that data down to its critical concepts based on your needs.

3. *Elaboration of Memories*

Filling the gaps is another thing that our brain does besides reducing information for easy comprehension and memorization. When you recall an event that's already happened, the cognitive processes elaborate on and reconstruct the memories. Often, we struggle to bring something to mind. In that case, the brain fills in the missing data with what fits.

4. *Interactions and Actions*

Cognition is about things going on inside our heads and how they influence the way we act. It involves:

a. Memories

b. Understanding of language

c. Knowledge of how the world works

d. Problem-solving abilities

So, our cognitive processes determine how we interact with the world.

Protecting Your Cognitive Abilities from the Effects of Aging

Most people hold the erroneous belief that aging causes us to lose all our cognitive abilities. And that this loss is inevitable. Research doesn't show that this is what happens. According to it, some areas of thinking undergo a decline with age while others remain stable. What's more, it's even slow down the age-imposed decline with certain interventions!

First, let's look at which areas are most affected by aging:

1. *Intelligence*

Knowledge and experience that we accumulate over time are called crystallized intelligence. Aging doesn't affect those. Instead, it brings a decline in abilities and intelligence that's fluid, i.e., not earned by experience or education.

2. *Memory*

There's also relative preservation of our remote memory, i.e., the recalling of past events. Newer memories that have just formed or are forming are more vulnerable to aging.

3. Attention

An older person is usually able to focus their attention on something, such as the TV. However, if they do that along with something else, i.e., multitask, they will find it difficult to divide their attention.

4. Language

Age doesn't affect one's verbal abilities, including their vocabulary. However, older individuals will be slower in getting words out or retrieving a specific term for something. You may recognize it from when your grandparents cannot recall the names of people or objects while engaged in conversation. While the information is still in their minds, the retrieval process becomes slower.

5. Reasoning/Problem Solving

Finding solutions for traditional problems and in conventional ways remains the same in older persons. Problems that you have not encountered before, on the other hand, will require extra time to figure out.

6. Processing Speed

Aging also affects the speed of cognitive and motor processes but not the processes themselves.

Keeping Your Brain Healthy and Young

1. *Physical Exercise*

It's official that exercise doesn't just improve your physical health; it also benefits the brain. In fact, according to various research studies, individuals who remain physically active are at a lower risk of developing Alzheimer's. They also decrease the chances of decline in mental function.

Mainly, exertion through exercise directs more blood flow to your brain. Consequently, your mental muscle gets more oxygen and nutrients – and quickly. The waste products, on the other hand, are also removed from the site more quickly.

Another way exercise could be helping slow down the effects of aging is by slowing down the natural reduction in brain connections. In some cases, exercising will even reverse the process!

In short, making a habit of exercising for half or one hour several times in a week can help your brain stay younger. You can choose any kind of activity that will get the heart rate up.

2. *Diet*

What you consume also plays a huge role in keeping your brain healthy. Most healthcare professionals deem the Mediterranean diet to be the best in this regard. That's because it consists of:

- Plant-based foods

- Healthy fats like olive oil
- Whole grains
- Fish

You'll notice that, unlike the typical American diet, this way of eating incorporates much less red meat. It's also low on salt, which comes with its own set of problems!

Back to mental wellness, there is research showing the Mediterranean diet reduces the likelihood of Alzheimer's disease. While more experiments are needed to figure out which of the diet's components are best for brain function, we do one thing. Omega fatty acids, like the ones you'll find in extra-virgin olive oil and other (healthy) fats, keep your brain's cells functioning properly. Not only that, they retard age-related decline in cognitive and mental focus.

3. *Alcohol*

Drinking affects our bodies in different ways as we age. You'll find out, though, that we don't believe in completely cutting out something from your life. Alcohol's no exception. So stick to the experts-recommended limit of one-two drinks per day for best results.

4. *Sleep*

Sleep is essential for brain health. Therefore, get between 7-8 hours of uninterrupted nap time daily. Substituting it with fragmented several-hour-long naps isn't as effective. Your brain needs the real consecutive thing to do its thing, i.e., consolidate and store memories.

During the process of consolidation, recent memories from different parts of the brain are reactivated and added to the store of long-term memories. The REM phase of your sleep helps stabilize those newly transformed memories. Thus, a well-established sleeping schedule is essential to your brain's well-being.

If you struggle with sleeping in long, continuous stretches, you may have sleep apnea. This disorder can be bad news for your brain's health, so seek professional help for it.

5. Mental Exercise

Just like any muscle, your brain can suffer from disuse. To keep it like the well-oiled machine that it is, keep it in use. Games like Sudoku and crossword puzzles are good for that purpose. If they're not to your liking, playing cards can act like cross-training sessions for the brain. Reading is another activity that keeps it busy. We'd advise switching between these pastimes for increased effectiveness.

Don't depend on the many paid brain-training programs that you'll find floating on the internet. Often, they make promises that they won't keep. Such programs also focus on memorization skills that won't help you in everyday life. In addition, watching TV or any streaming surface cannot replace the brain workout activities we've mentioned above. The former's a passive activity, which won't stimulate your brain!

6. Social Interactions

You may find it surprising that depression and stress can contribute to memory loss. Social interactions can help ward off those two disorders. So, schedule a time when you can connect with your loved ones and others. Doing so becomes even more necessary if you live alone.

Depression and stress both of which can contribute to memory loss. Look for opportunities to connect with loved ones, friends, and others, especially if you live alone. Brain shrinkage and atrophy are two processes that have been linked with social isolation! That means staying socially active will keep you smart.

The Link between Physical and Mental Health

So, aging affects our brain in various negative ways, that's for sure. But what does mental health have to do with our physical well-being?

Are They Connected?

Truthfully, the two facets of your health aren't as disconnected as you'd like to think. The connection between them has kept researchers busy for many decades. Right now, they do know that mental illness can have direct and indirect impacts on our physical health. We present several ways through which this can happen:

1. *Immune System and Depression*

It speaks to the importance of preventing depression, given that it's the most common mental disorder in Americans. The thing is, this disorder doesn't just alter your mood or motivation. It can also mount an attack on the immune system! When it suppresses T-cell responses, those defenders cannot act against the incoming bacteria and viruses. Consequently, you become more vulnerable to illness. You also will be sick for longer! Besides that, weaker immune systems are unable to curb the severity of allergies or asthma.

There's evidence of the reverse happening, too, i.e., stress-triggered immune systems driving someone towards depression! Chronic stress can trigger immune responses within your brain. In response, it begins an inflammatory response, which can act as the cause for depression.

An immune inflammation study links it to depression. Due to repeated stress, mice brains released cytokines – inflammation-related proteins. The release damaged the medial prefrontal cortex in mice. Since that's the part of the brain that can trigger depression, that's precisely what happened when it was destroyed!

The relationship between your immune system and depression is another confirmation that many health issues have both physical and mental elements. So, we should be focused on both!

2. Fatigue and Mood Disorders

People often don't understand the effects mood disorders can have on a person. A hallmark of these issues would be a persistent feeling of exhaustion. We may even think that it's only our brain making us feel as if we're tired. But that's not the case!

Mental exhaustion translates into physical fatigue. The participants were told to keep riding a stationary bike to the point of exhaustion. The study chose to define that as the point when participants couldn't keep up with 60 rpm for more than 5 seconds.

First, the participants underwent the test under usual conditions. Then, they were asked to complete a mentally stimulating task before they rode. As you'd expect them to be, the second situation caused exhaustion and listlessness in the participants. They were so tired they reached the point 15% earlier!

Now imagine how a persisting mental condition can stress out an individual physically. In reverse, someone chronically depressed/anxious is less likely to exercise. Even if they do engage in physical activity, they might quit early. Their interest might also flag when it comes to basic hygiene – and thus protection from disease.

3. Heart Health and Negative Emotions

We've already discussed what one should do about negative emotions. Now, let us look at how they affect our physical health, particularly our heart's. In an Australian study, acute feelings and their potential in causing heart attacks were monitored.

After an episode of intense anger, most people are in prime states for heart attacks! Spending two hours fuming over something can make the possibility of a heart attack almost nine times higher. The risk is close to 10 times for those struggling with intense anxiety. Anger and anxiety are also the two factors that make heart attacks likely at a young age!

Strengthening the Connection

So, now you understand how important it is to take steps to improve your mental health. Depression and other psychological disorders are bad news – in more ways than one! Here's what you can do to take care of your physical and mental health:

1. *Start with Self-Care*

Any steps you take to preserve or improve your current mental health or state comes under self-care. Such activities usually have two main functions. Firstly, they help you set up healthy boundaries. Secondly, they encourage you to find ways by which you can better cope with life's ups and downs.

If you're confused about where to start regarding self-care, we have some positive news for you. Most of the things you do to take care of yourself physically, like regular sleep schedules, interacting socially, and eating healthy, are also what you'd do for mental self-care.

In addition, we'd suggest looking for activities that let you pamper yourself. Select some that you can easily do on a regular basis. Sure, most of us would like to spend all our days languishing on an island somewhere. However, that might not be realistically possible. Therefore, aim lower. A beauty or skincare routine that leaves you feeling refreshed, for instance.

2. *Sleep Schedule*

As we've mentioned, an insufficient amount of sleep can exacerbate health problems. Now, let's discuss sleep scheduling. Harvard Medical School weighs in on the matter. They say that individuals with a history of insomnia are four times as much at risk of developing depression as those who don't. Conversely, close to 90 and more than 50 percent of people with depression and anxiety also have some kind of sleep disorder.

A well-regulated sleeping routine is even more critical for children. Insufficient sleep can weaken young immune systems. It may also affect the way their behavioral and mental states.

To resolve these issues, make sleep schedules. For kids, sleep routines involve:

- Having a concrete bedtime
- Drinking a glass of warm milk
- Restricting screen access an hour before bed

The same applies to adults, as well, although you can replace the milk with your favorite herbal tea blend. It's best to limit your screen access, as well.

3. *Going Outside*

Today, children and adolescents don't spend much time outside. The problem is even worse for us adults. That's doubly true for individuals with depression. That's because this disorder reduces the motivation to leave the house. The thing is that being around nature and getting out of your home can reduce the symptoms of depression.

Regardless of why you cannot go outside or if you have depression or not, you should schedule excursions. Two per week would be a good start. Whether you spend that time walking around the block or go to a park nearby, ensure you do it for 20 minutes at least. If you have kids in your care, get them to join you. Outside excursions are an actionable example that will improve their mental health as well.

4. *Scheduled Activities*

Another time-tested way that improves mental health *and* reduces the symptoms of depressions is working with your hands! When you do that, you keep half of your brain's cortex occupied. In a way, you're using your hands-on hobby to give your brain a good workout.

Of course, we don't mean for you to take up mechanical engineering or brain surgery to benefit from such an activity. Some alternatives that will do equally fine include:

- Art class
- Cooking
- Watercoloring
- Sewing
- Embroidery
- Bullet journaling
- Pottery
- Jewelry making
- Calligraphy

For children, too, an activity that mixes cognitive and physical aspects will ensure healthy brain development.

5. Treatment

A crucial part of self-care for excellent mental health limits your participation to seeking professional help. Some mental illness issues get worse if they're not worked out with qualified experts. A disorder that's disrupting your everyday life requires such immediate treatment. For that, we'd suggest looking for experts in counseling and dialectical behavioral therapy (DBT). Programs rooted in this therapy will address the disorder at the root. Sometimes, that's precisely what's needed.

Spark Forward – 3 Bite-sized Personal Interventions to Improve Matters of the Mind.

Don't Just Open Your Eyes -- Wake up Your Brain in the Mornings

Our four-step-long morning routine's simple: Drink water, put on some music, do light exercise, and take a cold shower. That's it; now you're ready for another morning!

Paying Attention to Inattentiveness

We all zone out and daydream. Since it's bound to happen, experts recommend scheduling your session! It will make you better at staying on task. In other words, when it doesn't matter, daydream as much as you can. Then, get back to the task at hand!

Putting Your Memory through its Paces

The more senses you involve to learn something, the more notice your brain will take of the activity. Consequently, it works harder at retaining the memory. So, select new-to-you activities that challenge all your senses. For example, guess the ingredients of a new dish. Or, if you try sculpt, focus on the feel and smell of the materials. And so on.

Chapter 2 - Body

"Keeping your body healthy is an expression of gratitude to the whole cosmos- the trees, the clouds, everything.

Thich Nhat Hanh

The Body of Evidence in Favor of Taking Care of Your Body

Of course, we already know the importance of staying fit physically. One main reason we should focus on physical fitness is that it affects all the aspects of our lives. Just try and pinpoint an area that it doesn't have an effect on. You can't, can you? So, the essential nature of being physically healthy cannot be overstated. Being inflexible, sluggish, and overweight only means you get to enjoy life a lot less.

But what does being physically fit even mean? It means having a strong core, so you can:

- Touch your toes
- Hike with your dog

- Jog for a couple of miles
- Walk up five flights of stairs

Living fully with a strong and energetic body comes with confidence and a better quality of life. In more specific terms and in keeping with the theme of this guide, this is why you should be physically fit:

Handle Stress and Be Able to Relax

Being physically fit by building muscle and increasing your flexibility makes you better able to handle stress. You'd be able to face higher levels of stress too. When you stretch taut muscles after a busy workday, you'd be relieving tension. Thus, when your body is at its peak, you will find it easier to relax.

While building muscle, you also burn stored fat. This fat is now available for energy production. So, by aiming for physical fitness, you get your metabolism to speed up and provide you with bursts of energy.

Save Money

About 90% of the money spent on healthcare in the US annually is done so on chronic mental and physical issues. Heart disease is responsible for one-third of American lives lost, while Alzheimer's is the sixth highest cause for fatality. Even though these chronic diseases cannot be prevented, you can reduce how at-risk you are for them. That mainly involves living a healthy life and making less risky choices, such as engaging in physical activity regularly. In short, when you look after your physical health, you save money you'd spend treating such illnesses!

Increase Your Life Expectancy

It's axiomatic that life expectancy increases with regular physical activity. The latter also minimizes the risk of premature mortality. While we cannot calculate by how many hours we can increase our life expectancy with such activity, it should be enough that exercise keeps us healthier and helps us live longer.

Reduce Your Risk of Injury

There's another advantage related to staying physical fitness. When we work out regularly, we also work towards increased:

- Muscle strength
- Stability
- Bone density
- Flexibility

In other words, physical fitness makes your body resilient to injury. Such hurts become familiar as you get older. So, strengthen your muscles and improve your balance so you'd be less likely to fall. And if you do take a tumble, suffering bone-based injuries would be less likely.

Improve Your Quality of Life

Living a sedentary life that lacks physical activity will take a toll on your bodies. Additionally, with a sedentary lifestyle, the chances of certain types of cancers also increase. The same is also true for mental health and chronic diseases. On the other hand, exercise-induced endorphins can lift your mood and safeguard your mental health.

Moreover, a healthy body opens the way to activities that would be otherwise out of your reach, such as hiking and deep-sea diving. Therefore, if you want to literally climb mountains, stay fit physically.

Stay Active

Ask a mountaineer why they do what they do. They'll tell you how rewarding an experience it is to reach that summit finally. On the way back, mountain climbers are wrapped up in a sense of accomplishment. Then there's also the spectacular scenery to consider. All such activities are a go for people with little to no fitness limitations.

But you don't need to surmount peaks to get that sense of achievement. Even a walk around the zoo with the family or spending time with your kids on the basketball court can be rewarding in itself. The only condition in such cases is that your body doesn't find such extensive physical activity challenging. Besides, if you cultivate this habit now, it should keep you on your toes even when you get older.

The Link between Your Mind and Body

The world today has a higher percentage of older adults. This has brought to attention the various factors responsible for their longevity. Many of these we're already familiar with, such as:

1. Health

2. General lifestyle
3. Genetic influences
4. Physical activity
5. Social relationships
6. Nutrition

Most researchers agree that centenarians are more vulnerable to and develop several chronic diseases. From a study about Danish centenarians, the following chronic illnesses were identified:

1. Cardiovascular disease
2. Dementia
3. Osteoarthritis
4. Ischemic heart disease
5. Hypertension

From another study, we find that only about 20% of older adults *escape* a diagnosis for common-age-related disorders.

Scientists also consider health to be one of the significant indicators for psychological well-being in that demographics. In short, the impact of their mental health on physical health matters as much in old age as it did before. However, there's also such a thing as subjective health that matters a lot. Subjective health refers to an individual's perception/evaluation of their own health. Often, it can be different from the interpretation of their objective health status.

While we're discussing subjective health, let's not forget that one's beliefs, attitudes, and motivations can determine the way they view their illness and disability. These and other individual differences shape the way we see our health.

They also play a crucial role in our psychological well-being as we age. For instance, our psychological characteristics will determine how willing and able we are to adapt to habits necessary for physical change. It is logical for scientists to use our psychological well-being as an indicator of aging-related successful adaptation. If it's negative, it's usually the consequence of maladaptive behavior. Psychological well-being reinforces appropriate behavior when positive.

The factors influencing our psychological well-being include:

1. Status of physical health

2. Socio-demographics, such as age, income, occupation, level of education, and social interaction

3. Marital status

4. Fiscal status

As you can see, our physical health has a role to play when considering psychological well-being in old age. Look at several ways by which it affects our mental health include:

1. As a source of life strain in adults – especially if they are dealing with a chronic disease

2. By lowering morale

3. Absence of stroke symptoms (positive effect)

4. Low cardiovascular risk (positive impact)

5. Better survival in old age (positive effect)

The results from such studies all demonstrate there's an association between perceived and objective health. Additionally, subjective health and long-standing chronic illness are even more strongly related in older adults. The diseases that influence our self-perceptions most commonly are:

- Heart conditions
- Asthma
- Joint complaints
- Chronic bronchitis
- Diabetes
- Back problems

Besides the connection with chronic illness, subjective health is also influenced by other health indicators. Those include:

1. How many meds an individual has to take

2. The number of times they have been hospitalized

3. How often they have to take a sick day

Thus, our emotional, mental, and physical well-being is related to our psychological health. If we have specific recurring physical symptoms or body sensations, it will affect what we think of our health. The same is true for our medical history, health beliefs, and behaviors.

You may have begun to see how your mental health is affected and influences your physical health. Let's now look at how it is connected with your spiritual well-being. Studies indicate unusual ways by which spiritual health affects mental health. For instance, a spiritually healthy person recovers from depression more quickly. That remained true for patients who didn't show any improvement in their physical function!

There's an extensive review that went through more than 800 studies about the association between spiritual thoughts and mental health. It concluded that those with spiritual health also experienced better mental health. In addition, these individuals also fared better in terms of successfully adapting to stress. From other analyses, we find out that higher spiritual health can also result in healthier bodies and lifestyles while reducing the need for medical care.

Reductions in the rate of depression and anxiety levels were also seen with daily spiritual activity. So much literature exists that also proves how spiritual health can improve the quality of life.

Your Body Talks – What We Aren't Asking You to Do

Most of us have promised ourselves that we'll start eating healthy. For many, that's their new and shiny New Year's promise. For others, it's a recurring goal they fail to achieve. Truthfully, it is too easy to slip back into adapting less healthy eating routines. What we don't consider is that the best of intentions won't help us out in this. If you're going to make an attempt, ensure you do so with the best information. By that, we mean the knowledge that would support you in this change.

One very crucial detail that we overlook is how much the little things matter. You may be choosing an eating plan that's going to ensure you lose weight. Or, you may be addressing a health problem, such as high blood pressure, with the proper nutrition, such as a low-salt diet. Either way, it's those seemingly insignificant things that you should be watching out for. Why? Because they're what throw you off track!

Don't buy it? Well, let's see if you've neglected one – or all – of the things we mention below. Along with the common mistakes, we also give you tips on how you can avoid or correct them:

1. Think in Terms of a Diet and Not Nutrition

Before you grab the new-and-diet-friendly grocery list items, let's get one thing straight. If you start off thinking that you're starting a diet, you're on the fast road towards failure! You already know how much a mindset influences behavior. So, instead of dieting, think in terms of nutrition and eating habits.

Why, you ask? What makes the two so different? A diet is something that people will adopt for a limited duration. You, too, will do it for a week, a month, or until you've achieved your objective. Then, you'll give up eating the way your diet plan instructs you to. It means you'll revert to the ways that made you physically unfit in the first place.

With a dieting mentality, the best you can expect is yo-yo dieting. The weight loss it brings about will not last. In addition, dieting doesn't bring about lasting health improvements, either.

So, tell yourself that you *have* a diet but don't have *to* diet. Then make sure the steps you take improve your *actual* diet. Transform your existing lifestyle so the changes you make become part of your daily life.

2. Not Lift the Right Weight Off Your Shoulders

Puny weights, such as the 2-pounders, will fit into your desk drawer perfectly. They can even help you build muscle – in the long run. However, what they won't be doing is provide a lot of resistance. Improving strength becomes more complex in such cases. If you want to get anywhere, you'd need to do many more reps. Now, imagine trying to squeeze a lot of exercise in the tiny window you get before attending Weekly Meeting 8,473. Doesn't seem too likely, does it?

To fix it, incorporate some compound exercises into your sessions. Look for the ones that are going to engage multiple muscle groups simultaneously. Pushups and squats are two excellent examples of such compound exercises. When you do these, your body weight becomes the source of resistance – a much better one than the small weights you were using before. In addition, the more groups of muscles you can engage, the higher you can get your heart rate. Consequently, you'll be burning more calories.

For people who'd like to use equipment, we'd recommend aiming for the TRX and Urbnfit. Portable, adjustable, smaller sized, and multipurpose when it comes to incorporating into various exercises.

3. Do It Right and Ensure Your Stomach Devours Itself

Any diet that restricts food too drastically is bad news. The first thing that such diets do is bring your metabolic rate down. You're already not providing your body with suitable fuel in simple terms, i.e., by not eating. Since it cannot depend on the incoming food for energy production, your body will go into panic mode. Your brain will order it to conserve all the stored fat in starvation mode. Clearly, you're weathering a drought or lack of food – or that's what your brain would think. And it will try to reserve the stores of fat for even worse emergencies!

Plus, there are cravings that we must deflect too. In the end, most of us will go on a donut or burger binge and do more damage than if we'd continued eating normally.

The fix for this issue is to pay attention to the hunger quotient. Base your meals on it and consume fat and protein-rich foods in sufficient quantity to satisfy the cravings. Listen to what your body's saying, and you'll end up healthier.

4. Forget to Exercise Your Right to Different Exercises

Going through the same routine can become like second nature. Such familiarity makes you feel safer and breeds warm, fuzzy feelings within you. There's only one issue, though. Your body is a self-learning and high-functioning machine. So, if you keep walking it through the same paces, it will find a way to adapt to those exercise moves!

Consequently, your workout sessions will be anything but challenging for your body with passing time. In the end, you'll plateau. And since those moves have become habitual, you'll feel tempted to disengage from them as well mentally. Boredom and loss of the fitness mindset won't help matters. You also risk injury if you adopt a crappy form, what with your attention wandering during the sessions.

A workable solution would be to maintain logs of the exercises you've completed. In addition, read up on the basic muscle groups, including your back and chest and biceps and triceps. Then choose exercises that benefit a different muscle group per week. Keep rotating and switching. Besides this, your aim should be not to repeat exercises for the muscle groups in the second round of rotation.

Bring in even more diversity by shifting the overall program after every month or two. For instance, do kickboxing for a month and then go for yoga. Replace that with Tabata, and then go for the aerobic step next. For people with an unusually brief window into which they fit exercise, varying the location each time can keep things interesting. For example, go from your desk to a chair in the break room.

5. Say Yes! To All Fruits

Any good diet would incorporate a lot of whole natural foods, and that includes fruits. However, limiting your fruit intake is necessary if you want to lose weight. That's because fruits are full of different nutrients and fiber – most of which are good for us. However, they also contain truckloads of fructose – a sugar! Our body is very receptive to fructose's arrival and digests it quickly.

So, while fruit is a healthier alternative for when the cravings hit you. Reach for them instead of munching on other desserts. But they are also not a *free* food. People who want to lose weight would need to limit fruit intake to 1-2 servings per day. Substitute with raw veggies, like carrots and cucumber.

6. Stop… Just Yet!

Indeed, you don't have to do all your exercise at the same time. However, if you don't keep up the hard work for even 10 minutes, your heart rate doesn't go up enough. If that doesn't happen, you don't gain the maximum benefits associated with exercise!

So, what you can do is stop inserting flash cardio and single sets into the brief window when you get some downtime. Instead, dedicate the entirety of your lunch break to exercise. Can't manage that? Then schedule gym time before or after work.

7. Think Calories Are Calories

Not all of them amount to the same thing. Sure, you shouldn't over-consume them. In addition to that, you should also remember they aren't all equal. Don't waste time counting every calorific intake, though. After all, various factors can influence how many of those we eat every day. Stress, social schedule, emotions, hormones, and cravings will cause the quantity to vary.

Moreover, the type of food we reach for and how our bodies process it will also affect what we consume. For instance, eating a meal that amounts to 100 calories can have different outcomes, depending on if the food is jelly beans vs. slices of turkey breast and avocado.

Say you eat three cookies instead of two but maintain your daily calorie goal. That isn't smart because it will work against you in the long run. Additionally, you also won't be meeting your nutrient needs.

8. Not Dress for the Occasion

Wearing a skirt and heels to the gym wouldn't be a smart move. You'd be flashing everyone every time you do downward dog! Likewise, pulling on tight-fitting dress slacks won't do you any favors. Particularly when you have to whip some squats in them.

Dressing correctly will most likely entail wearing something business casual that's looser. With all that freedom of movement, you'd be able to breathe easily while working out. Pick a fabric that's breathable and easy-to-launder. If you can choose simple-to-remove and put back on layers, you won't dread the thought of squeezing your body into your workout clothes. Finally, store your workout shoes under your desk – if you go to the gym after/before work.

9. Eat More Because Low-Fat Means Healthier Food

Don't relax your guard just because the labels on edible products claim they are low-fat. If the manufacturers were honest, they'd put this on the labels instead: *low-fat and added sugar*. We've evolved to find fatty foods tasty because they are high-energy. Early man didn't shovel bowl after bowl into their bodies while sitting on a couch. Their bodies could take the nourishment from fatty foods because meals like that weren't common occurrences.

But that's not how things are for us. While we lost the neanderthal lifestyle, our preference remains the same. Nowadays, when manufacturers take out the fat, they make up for it with additives, fillers, and sugars. That's to keep the taste mostly the same.

The fix for this problem is to go for the real version of the food you're craving. If you like peanut butter, eat the homemade version. Alternatively, buy the store-bought bottle that say contains peanuts and forego those claiming to be low on fat.

10. Take Gluten to Be the Root of All Evil

Once it was thoroughly vilified in the press, gluten became the reason so many celebs lost weight. You may also be wishing for a gluten-free lifestyle so you can join their ranks and experience weight loss.

Think about it, though. You'd be saying goodbye to cakes, breads, cookies, and refined pastas. This is the main reason people lose weight drastically in a gluten-free lifestyle. Such an approach comes with some issues. For one, the efforts you make might not match the results produced.

Secondly, abandoning gluten completely to reap weight loss benefits isn't even necessary! Any healthy diet should already have a higher proportion of veggies and fruits. Lean protein, low-gluten grains, and healthy fats also form part of such a diet.

Finally, if you take out the gluten only to replace it with processed foods with high amounts of unhealthy additives, you'd only be doing more harm!

11. Take a Number

Getting caught up with the number your scale shows every morning is a bad idea. It may even be counterproductive. Imagine the weight gain you see in those numbers is due to your body gaining more muscle and not fat. Then think how much it would suck if you just saw the digits and gave up. You'd also be saying bye to a healthier bod!

In short, don't use the scale to weigh yourself at all. Pick your favorite and formerly-comfy pair of skinny jeans. Or, aim to fit into your little black dress the way you used to. Then hide the scale from your eyes and focus on eating healthy. In addition, train yourself to eat like that consistently and not just when on a diet.

Aside from these measures, there's one more thing you can do. Stay realistic when it comes to excluding foods that are too fatty or packed with carbs. For example, vowing no more donuts are going to pass through your lips is unrealistic. It may also make you cave into your cravings much faster. To prevent that, indulge in a reasonable treat occasionally. Don't be only restrictive without paying attention to sustainability.

For success in the long haul, it's crucial that your new plan be an eating plan as opposed to a diet plan. It will be easier to continue the former and turn it into a lifelong commitment. Don't deprive yourself of certain nutrients or even types of foods. Pick treats that match your daily sugar and calorie allowances. The AHA considers 24 and 36g for women and men to be safe for daily consumption.

12. Kick Out the Wrong Foods

Many of us avoid certain healthy foods because we assume they are bad for us. For instance, it is okay to avoid trans-fat, which is present in most packaged foods. The main reason for that is it raises the levels of bad LDL cholesterol and triglycerides while doing the opposite for the good or HDL cholesterol. In the same way, we shouldn't consume unlimited quantities of saturated fat – an important part of red meat and butter. Any processed and packaged foods are laden with trans fats, salt, and sugar. So, we should stay away from those too.

However, we should cut out healthy fats from our lives completely. Sure, they pack more calories in a gram as compared to carbs or proteins. But your heart won't be the same without the greasy care of unsaturated fats! Replace saturated fats with these and reduce LDL and total cholesterol amounts. To get at healthy fats, you'd need to eat more:

1. Seeds

2. Avocados
3. Nut butters
4. Olive oil
5. Nuts

Additionally, fruits are nature's way of treating us to something. As we mentioned before, you should make them a part of daily nutrition. As long as you remember, they also have sugar and eat fruits in moderation, you'll do fine. Remember that the way your body handles natural and added sugar is different. Most fruits also have quite a lot of fiber, vitamins, and antioxidants. Many of them take us closer to our weight loss and fitness goals. For instance, berries are good for weight loss and heart health.

13. Stock the Pantry with Unhealthy Foods Within Reach

Avoiding unhealthy foods will take more work if you keep stocking your pantry with them! Why make it that much more challenging, even if they are there for special occasions? Throw them out and restock the shelves with healthier food. That's so when you're craving a snack and end up in the pantry, and you will be grabbing a healthy snack. However, if your hands can get to a half-gallon tub of ice cream, most of the dessert will end up in your tummy!

Another good tip is to arrange matters so you'll have to go out and get any dessert at the time you're craving it. Not buying it well in advance will work in your favor. After all, we don't feel like going out all the time. Hurray for human laziness!

14. Eat at Night

Many of us will scoop spoonful after spoonful of food into our mouths while we watch TV or a streaming service. First of all, eating at night creates trouble. Secondly, when our concentration is otherwise occupied, we tend to overeat. Thirdly, saving up calories from the daytime to consume them at night is also unhealthy. Your body is expending energy during the day, and it's going to need those calories to keep working.

Additionally, if you starve yourself all day, you might overeat at night. Then there's the matter of heartburn. That's a near certainty if you eat close to bedtime. Heartburn will disrupt your sleep too! In short, nightly meals are a bad idea.

To prevent all of this from becoming an issue, we suggest rethinking the timing of your meals. Should you notice that you always feel snackish during the night, then grab a handful of nuts or some slices of fruits. Just ensure that you add that to your daily calorie consumption plan. Aside from that, start spacing out your calories in the daytime too!

15. Not Track Your Food Intake

While we'll advise against obsessive tracking down of every morsel of food you eat, we do advise that you monitor your intake. It increases the chances of meeting the goal you have in mind – whether it's weight loss or monitoring sodium for your blood pressure.

Here's why that's true: you create an awareness of what you're putting in your mouth on a regular basis. You also realize how much you're eating of each type of food. Consequently, figuring out what works for your body and what doesn't becomes easier. For instance, insufficient food during the day may be forcing you to overeat at night. After all, your body *must* fulfill its requirements in one way or another!

Maintain an honest-to-god food diary or via a digital app can solve such problems. For digital solutions, you might like to check out My Fitness Pal or the USDA Food Tracker.

How You Can Improve – Different Tips for People at Different Levels of Physical Fitness

Making certain mistakes can prevent both experienced individuals and those who are new to exercise from making progress. We mention tips for you that will help score more results during your strength training sessions. The best part is we've included advice for all -- newbies, intermediates, and advanced workout goers. So, you can try the ones specifically directed at you, or you can attempt them all!

For Beginners

What to Do During Exercise

- **Keep Moving Each Day**. If you're a beginner, it's essential that you form a habit. That will take exercising on all seven days of the week! While this is a good thing for consistency, we'd recommend you don't overwhelm yourself right off the bat. Start with only daily 30 minutes of cardio and strength training twice a week. Keep at this for two to three months. Once you can feel the moves becoming ingrained in your mind's eye, it may be time for a new routine!

- **Don't Tense Up.** Beginners will often tense up when they work out. You may be doing it due to a determination to lose weight. Or, you could be lacking confidence. Either way, loosen up! First, because you're wasting energy as you hold on to the bike's bars with whitened knuckles. Secondly, you can put all that energy to good use by focusing it on the muscles you're working out. Loosening up will produce better results.

What Not to Do During Exercise

- **Only Remember the Treadmill.** Those who are new to exercise often remain stuck to the treadmill or do the same routine every time. As mentioned above, variety is quite necessary if you want your body to view these sessions as challenges. Should your body find a way to adapt to the moves in a workout, you'd get bored or even hurt! In addition, when a workout becomes easier for you, you may be thinking it's due to your uber-fit state. So, keep mixing up things – even if you do it by varying time and intensity. Switching between the bike and an outdoor jogging session every now and then can keep things interesting!

- **Slouch Your Way to Places.** By that, we refer to your posture, of course. Whether you're sitting down and leafing through a magazine or curling dumbbells, make sure your posture is right! You see, it's not just about your performance. Your posture also affects your mood! A slouched position probably indicates that you've checked out of your workout – mentally and physically. That increases the chances of injuries.

  When you're slumped down like that, you don't breathe as deeply, either. All your muscles are working at total capacity during a sweat session. They need that breath of fresh air to keep doing so. So, look for posture-straightening exercises that you can employ within workouts.

For Regular Exercisers

What to Do During Exercise

- **Setting Up New Goals.** Gym regulars often hit slumps. During such a phase, they will find it difficult to keep seeing the benefits of exercising regularly. To them, it doesn't even seem fun anymore, which is they lose the thing that kept them motivated in the past. If that's happening to you, check yourself as soon as you begin dodging gym dates!

  Then, preferably before it even becomes an issue, find a new challenge. Whether you do that by going on an activities-packed vacation or sign up for a 5K, just do it!

- **Learn to Breathe Better and Not Just Easier.** Focusing on your breathing can help you improve your performance! So, when you arrive at the rest phases of your session, inhale deeply. Then, when you reach the work phases, exhale forcefully – it will help generate more force and keep you going for longer. Do both, i.e., inhaling and exhaling, to a count of three.

Exercise Tips for Fitness Devotees

What to Do During Exercise

What You're Not Good at. Often, advanced exercisers won't attempt challenging exercises just because they aren't good at those. Only doing exercises you're naturally good at can put you at a disadvantage, i.e., it prevents you from building a stronger and more balanced body. The challenging exercises will also prevent overuse injuries. So, whether it's squats, stretches, or crunches, stop avoiding them. Make these moves a part of your routine at least twice to three times a week.

Working Out with Others, More Relaxed Partners. You may think that somebody who moves at a more leisurely pace has nothing to teach you. But you'd be wrong! Try partnering with them once a week and see what we mean. Slower, relaxed workouts help your body regenerate. They may also be fun to do every once in a while because of the sedate pace and the company! Failing to take this measure is why fitness fanatics often experience a higher injury rate. Your body shouldn't be pushed to its limits during each session. Doing easier sessions periodically allows your muscles time for repair. They will have become stronger by the time your next workout approaches.

What Not to Do During Exercise

Forget to Go Unplugged Every So Often. If you let your mind be set on the numbers, you forget to listen to what your body is actually telling you. Sure, tracking your heart rate and running rate can provide valuable feedback instantly. However, obsessing over these metrics will keep you from enjoying exercise. At times, looking down at those digits might even cause you to keep pushing your body, although you know you're not feeling 100%! So, don't forget to workout in unplugged mode every once in a while. Exercise at a feel-good pace and listen to your body's cues for an enjoyable experience.

Beat the Olympians at Eating. Indeed, top athletes require massive amounts of energy bars and sugary sports drinks in response to the caloric demands of the sports they participate in. It's likely that you aren't an athlete on the playing field. If you only workout to stay healthy and not to become the next Ironman, limit those two fuel sources. Three balanced meals along with two light snacks will do fine for you. You don't need to down a carb bar and energy drink – 300 calories each – after each session. Be careful when picking those snacks, too. Fruit and crackers are always better choices over anything immensely sugar-laden!

Spark Forward – 3 Bite-sized Personal Interventions to Improve Matters of the Body

Plan for Obstacles

One of the main reasons we skip workouts is because we don't have a plan for when we'll come up against an obstacle. For instance, can you plan an alternative workout for when you're stuck inside due to rain? No equipment available? Figure out how to substitute stair-climbing in your impromptu session! Been skipping gym because you don't want to get your work clothes sweaty? Start packing a change of clothes! And so on.

Switch to Cast Iron

Surprisingly with this move, you'll do two things. Boost your iron intake, so your muscles enjoy more oxygen. And, two, avoid the carcinogenic substances found in non-stick pan coating.

Stretch the Truth

A good stretch does wonders when done as the first thing after waking up. Just dedicate ten minutes to it making your body lose its stiffness due to being immobile for so long. Easy exercises, such as the single-knee hugger, can even be done while you lay on your back! Keep your left leg down while raising the right toward your chest. Wrap hands around the right hamstring while you pull on the

Chapter 3 - Spirit

Where the spirit does not work with the hand, there is no art!

Leonardo da Vinci

Religion vs. Spirituality

These two terms may seem synonymous to you, but they aren't! A person can be highly spiritual without also being religious. Before we discuss the many advantages of spirituality, let us first differentiate between religion and spirituality.

When it comes to religion, it's something that operates based on faith and intuition. It's not based on reason and focuses on what exists beyond the visible world. Spirituality, though, is an internal process. It helps you seek personal authenticity and wholeness, so you'll understand who you really are.

The idea on which most religions are based centers around a single or a group of beings. This entity is transcendental, so it has created the world and governs it. Thus, the world and everyone in it owes their destiny to the said entity. Instead of the beings, some religions may follow an eternal principle. In spirituality, a practitioner seeks to transcend their own current locus of centricity.

Religions are constructs that are usually agreed upon by specific people or sects. They consist of beliefs and practices. They posit that the evolution of the rituals, conducts, and principles occur naturally as the followers respond to belief. Religions also concern themselves with things like the afterlife.

Spiritualism, on the other hand, lets an individual develop a greater connectedness to themselves and others. It helps them find meaning and direction in life. Spirituality encourages people to explore their relationship with an intangible but pervasive power. Whether it's an essence or central value, this power exists outside human knowing.

Comparing the Two

It may seem to you from the definitions that the two overlap a lot. However, that's not true even though both religion and spirituality concern themselves with what exists beyond the corporeal, visible, and rational universe. In a way, they provide us with tools to get at what lies beyond our physical world.

Maybe what's beyond it is a supreme being, but the way religion and spirituality look at that entity is different. For religion, there are no two ways about the existence of the said entity. In spirituality, there's a tentativeness about just whom or what that is. Some spiritually-advanced people may call that being God – if the former's religious. Those who are non-religious and still spiritually developed may have no need or means to define what that entity could be.

So, spirituality doesn't concern itself with issues of deity and divine power. That's where religion comes in.

Other apparently overlapping areas occur that are actually different. One of them is the focus on activity. Religions focus on action embodied within exercises, rituals, and prayers. The spirituality descriptors are more about the connotations of action and movement. You might even be familiar with some of these:

- Process
- Developing
- Transcending
- Deriving
- Exploring

Additionally, religion can exist independently of the individual practicing it, but that is not so for spirituality. That's because the former is an external process while spirituality is perpetually internal. Even when someone moves outward from themselves and transcends or finds connectedness to others and themselves and strikes a relationship with what lies beyond the knowable world, they're not necessarily doing it externally. In a way, their inner world is expanding, so it can include the outer world!

On the one hand is religion, a public search for meaning, wholeness, transcendence, and purpose. On the other is spirituality, which is a more personal search of these things. It is also an apprehension of the essence that animates the core of life, i.e., the spirit.

Why Practice a Form of Spirituality?

Spiritual Communities Improve Life

Spiritual fellowship is encouraged as a tradition in some communities. As traditions go, attending a meditation group together can benefit you in the long run. When you attend the sessions with the same group of people, you'll form ties of social support. Having them may increase the sense of belonging, community, and security you feel. We've already mentioned how helpful strong relationships can be for our continued well-being and bolstering life expectancy. Participating regularly can also improve your mood and health.

Spiritual Strength is Helpful in Overcoming Hardships

People overcome trauma in different ways. Some of us cannot deal with having experienced incidents of abduction, war, and imprisonment without seeking comfort in religion. Others opt for spirituality. While the two are drastically different, they behave in the same manner in such cases. Spiritually-advanced people use their knowledge to find ways that allow them to meet the challenge. Once dealt with, the people can continue with their lives purposefully. In other words, spiritual strength – religious or otherwise – helps them bounce back and carry on!

With a strong spiritual outlook, people can also find meaning in the difficult circumstances they face in life. To them, such trying times can seem like opportunities for personal development. Another aspect of spiritual practice is that it helps people recognize how everything in life is interconnected. This knowledge buffers the pain for them when they encounter difficulties. For instance, when you fail at something, you shouldn't let your experience isolate you. Instead, through spirituality, you'll see how that very encounter makes you a part of the shared human experience. So, failing doesn't isolate you. Instead, it helps you see the togetherness that comes from countless others having undergone a similar hardship. The blow that life just dealt you softens!

Spiritual People are Better at Making Healthier Choices

By adhering to spiritual traditions, you may enjoy another health benefit, albeit an indirect one. Since spirituality requires treating your body with kindness and avoiding any unhealthy behaviors, you'd be doing the same. Such tenets can often exclude smoking, drinking, committing crimes, or violence from a spiritual person's life. Instead, you'll be practicing preventative habits, such as taking vitamins and wearing seatbelts. Thus, expect your life to become much healthier due to spirituality!

Spirituality Increases Longevity

From this exhaustive review, it becomes clear that both spirituality and religiousness are more successful at reducing mortality as compared to other health interventions. The difference is more than significant, i.e., the two can bring about an 18% reduction! The life-lengthening benefits that religion and spirituality produce are comparable to healthy habits, like:

- Eating a diet high in fruits and veggies
- Taking blood pressure meds

Besides studies suggest people who participate in spiritual practices regularly tend to live longer, there's also research on what might be causing the longevity. In this study, we learn about interleukin (IL)-6 – one of the possible mechanisms. When we're at increased risk of disease, the IL-6 levels increase as well. We learn that the 1700 older participants who attended church had half as much a chance of having elevated IL-6levels! Possible reasons that the authors suggest include improved stress control due to:

- Better coping mechanisms
- Strong personal values
- Rich social support
- Well-formed worldview

Spirituality Teaches You Forgiveness

You cannot possibly hope to grow as a person without learning how to forgive. Whether it's for yourself or others, forgiveness refers to letting go of blame and negative feelings in the aftermath of a hurtful incident. Besides helping you transcend pettiness, forgiveness also carries health benefits. Some of those are:

- Stronger immunity
- Healthier cardiovascular system
- Longer lifespan
- Lower blood pressure

Spirituality Acts Like a Coping Mechanism

Patients who are spiritually advanced could be utilizing their beliefs to cope with illness, pain, and other life stresses. There's evidence that spirituality gives people a more positive outlook and improves life's quality. For example, life satisfaction was higher for patients with advanced cancer if they were also spiritual. Both religious and non-religious patients seemed in less pain and happier. Spirituality is also used to measure the quality-of-life scores. It indicates that spiritually-progressive patients with advanced disease experienced the following:

- A meaningful personal existence
- Life goals fulfillment
- Life satisfaction

Spirituality also has a role to play when it comes to pain management. In a study, spiritual well-being increased a patient's ability to enjoy their life. That was true even as they dealt with the pain. It makes spirituality an important clinical target. The American Pain Society's questionnaire was distributed amongst hospitalized patients. The surveyors wanted to know which non-drug method helped patient pain management. More patients put their faith in personal prayer than they did in pain meds and injections, massages, etc.

Spirituality is also instrumental for patients coping with imminent death or disease. In one case, 93% of 108 women with gynecologic cancer stated it was the main way they coped. In 90 HIV-positive patients, spiritual activity decreased fear of death and guilt.

Spirituality Speeds up Recovery

A spiritual commitment may also enhance the rate of recovery from illnesses and surgery. In one case, heart transplant patients were better at complying with follow-up treatments if they also participated in spiritual activities and considered their religious beliefs to be an essential part of their lives. During their annual follow-up visit, these patients exhibited:

- Higher self-esteem levels
- Improved physical functioning
- Fewer health worries
- Less anxiety

Generally, people who worry less tend to fare better when it comes to health outcomes. It may be that being spiritually open enhances this quality and enables people to live more in the present moment.

Similarly, spirituality is linked to two other positive traits for some patients, i.e., the power of hope and that of positive thinking. The placebo effect is well-documented in medical science. Renamed "remembered wellness," it can also be seen as a patient tapping into their inner resources and healing ability. For instance, in a study, between 16-60% of patients showed improvement from various illnesses when the researchers gave them a placebo. They were receiving *treatments* for a variety of issues, such as:

- Pain
- Seasickness
- Common cold
- Cough
- Headaches

- Drug-induced mood change

According to Dr. Herbert Benson's book, the patient-physician relationship can also exert a placebo effect. So, what makes placebos so effective that they can influence the health outcome of a patient? Whether in the form of a pill or as the relationship with their physician, patients can benefit from placebos due to their positive beliefs.

Besides the placebo effect, Dr. Herbert Benson was also involved in research on how specific spiritual practices can affect patient health. It began when people approached him and requested he figure out whether transcendental meditation had any health benefits to offer. Unsurprisingly, he found that by meditating twice a day for just 10-20 minutes, people can experience the following benefits:

- Decreased metabolism
- Slower heart rate
- Slower brain waves
- Decreased rate of respiration

Calling it the relaxation response, Dr. Herbert Benson discovered that meditation is beneficial in the treatment of various ailments, including:

- Chronic pain
- Infertility
- Insomnia
- Premenstrual syndrome

- Anxiety
- Depression
- Hostility

What's more, meditation also proved a useful adjunct for HIV and cancer patients – as we've mentioned above. According to Benson, if stress worsens a patient's condition suffering from an illness, meditation acts as an effective therapy and helps them relax.

Ask healthcare professionals, and they'll tell you close to 60-90% of patients visit a primary care office because of stress-related issues. Practicing the relaxation response helps them control or reduce the intensity of symptoms in cases of high blood pressure, irritable bowel syndrome, chronic pain, and headaches. If it's true for them, it could likely benefit you too. The best part? That it doesn't take long to get into the relaxation response. Once you learn it, try to practice it at home, at work, and with your healthcare provider. The more frequently you do that, the fewer visits you'll be making to the doctor for most stress-related issues!

Spirituality can Strengthen the Immune System

The human body is intelligently built, so it knows how and when to heal itself. However, this natural ability to heal can become blocked due to various reasons. Spiritual practices, such as meditation and mindfulness, can remove that blockage. Since they trigger the body's healing ability, they can encourage it to return to a state of balance.

In one University of California study, we see how spirituality helped HIV-positive patients. When they meditated, they experienced a slower rate of decline in their immune cell counts. From another piece of research, we see that mindfulness meditation affects the brain and immune functions in positive ways.

Spirituality can Lower Risk of Depression

We know that spirituality encourages its practitioners to explore their inner worlds. This type of journey can help people connect more deeply with themselves and others. Crucial to our mental health is finding that kind of connection. And, since our bodies and minds are interconnected, the healthier we are mentally, the better it is for our physical wellbeing.

More specifically, spirituality can help with stress-related depression. It's common among people who deal with chronic illness, disability, or pain on a regular basis. As evidence, let us look at the results of a study done at the University of Alabama Medical Center. A hundred patients who were to receive cardiac surgery were part of this research. Close to 95 percent of them said they prayed, while 70 percent found prayer as a helpful pre-op coping mechanism.

Additionally, mental illnesses are often rooted in the absence of meaningful connections. That can lead to loneliness. Mindfulness-Based Stress Reduction or MSBR is the specific spiritual practice that is effective in countering such loneliness and the expression of the pro-inflammatory genes.

Spiritual and Stress Reduction

It is natural to feel a certain amount of stress. All of us experience it and live with it ably. However, chronic stress can give rise to health issues. Many meditation-based studies and how it affects stress exist. And, while spiritual practices, such as meditation, yoga, and walking, can help manage stress and help you remain positive, they are just one aspect of the solution. There's no one answer to the question of chronic stress because none of our sides, mental, physical, and spiritual, exist independently. Thus, it's better to take into account all things that will help you maintain a good life. That includes eating healthy food, staying physically active, and opening yourself to spirituality.

Spirituality and Blood Pressure

Stress is basically your body receiving help from your brain to fight off a situation that's causing disruption. This help arrives in the form of an increased flow of blood that's rich in hormones, which will help you achieve that. In short, to fight off the stressor, your body will increase the blood pressure, narrow the blood vessels, thus, making your heart beat faster so it can pump more blood. While this is a natural response if you experience it once in a while, repeated exposure to stress leads to elevated blood pressure and hypertension.

Lowering blood pressure is possible through spiritual practices. Doing so helps heal your physical body, but it also provides you with mental and emotional support. As we've mentioned before, it isn't enough to just consider the physical symptoms when you're unwell. Complete healing can only happen when you also factor in the mental and emotional aspects. So, you'll have to consider the actual cause of the stress you're facing. And there's no better way to do it than by exploring the realms of your inner space deeply. What can help you tap into that space? Spirituality!

From a study by James A. Anderson PhD, we can discover the potential of transcendental meditation in helping control blood pressure. Both systolic and diastolic blood pressure exhibited a decrease as a result of this practice!

Spirituality may Help you Sleep Better

Restful sleep is crucial for maintaining good health. Yet, so many of us find it difficult to make that happen. Whether it's your lifestyle choices or habits, something may be interfering with your sleep schedule and causing chronic sleep problems. Sometimes, the issue is stress-related and is connected to a major transition, life event, or trauma that you may be undergoing. Regardless of what's keeping you from a restful sleep, you should work to restore your body's sleep-wake cycle and its natural rhythm.

When you meditate, you calm the turbulence within. Consequently, you sleep better. Moreover, if you're no longer carrying your mental or emotional baggage with you when you go to bed, your body is able to heal itself physically. Spiritual practices, including yoga, journaling, meditation, and exercise, help you process the stress of the day in a healthy way. Therefore, you won't be under its effects when you hit the bed.

These were just some of the health benefits that you'll experience when you're spiritually open. What's more, the positive effects are long-lasting. Remember that you don't have to demonstrate how spiritual you are to anybody. Find out which type of practice works for you and engage in it privately. We provide some ideas on how to do that below.

What are Some Areas of Practice?

The kind of practice someone takes up depends on the goal they have. Therefore, it's possible for you to reach that goal by walking different spiritual paths. For instance, consider the following examples of goals and the approaches one may take to arrive at them:

Religious Spiritualism

- Buddhism is best for people who desire to achieve enlightenment and the cessation of suffering. It's for you if you want to rid yourself of mental defilements and see the truth for what it is

- Sufism lets the practitioner experience divine revelation when they surrender and serve God

- Through Christian mysticism, too, you can experience union with God

- Daoism and Taoism practitioners live in harmony with the Dao. They cultivate all aspects of selves and sublimate the energy.

- With Kabbalah, a practitioner can learn the ultimate laws of the universe, find who they are and who the Creator is.

- Jainism is the journey that leads one to become a perfected being. It's about liberation, purification, and salvation.

Spiritualism

However, as we've mentioned before, you don't have to be religious to be spiritual. Here are other ways that will take you to where you need to go:

- Yoga purifies the mind and helps unite your soul with that of the universe's. Through it, you can find liberation or moksha. Once united with the universe or absolute consciousness, you become your true self.

- Vedanta is about realizing your true self too. It helps you get rid of your ego so that you can achieve pure consciousness of body and mind.
- Shamanism is all about living in harmony with nature. When you practice it, you work with invisible forces. Your goal becomes the spiritual welfare of others and, through it, you heal your own soul.

As evident, spiritual practice exists across multiple traditions. However, all those traditions-based ways can be divided into practices that support:

- Personal cultivation, exploration, and sublimation
- Learning, absorbing, and understanding
- External action

Cultivation, Exploration, and Sublimation

Meditation

Controlling your attention is what meditation is all about. It can also be divided into more subcategories based on the eventual goal. If you concentrate at a single point, you're practicing focused attention. However, if you're becoming aware of what you're experiencing in the present moment, then you're doing open monitoring. For pure awareness type of meditation, your attention remains unengaged and undistracted from your consciousness.

Prayer

It's a part of most theistic paths. Simply put, when you pray, you direct your mind to the Divine. This exercise is about devotion and surrender. You can use a scripted prayer or go with a spontaneous one. Pray loudly or quietly. There's also pure communion, which happens without words.

Breath & Energy Exercise

Specific ways to breathe and move our attention through our body form these exercises. Some visualization or repetition of sounds often accompanies them. Their original purpose is to heal, calm, and energize the doer. An example from yoga would be the pranayama, while the qigong from Daoism is another. You can also use them to prep for meditation, which is subtler and more internal.

Somatic Techniques

For various purposes, such as developing health or freeing the flow of energy, some techniques use body movements or postures along with breathwork. In yoga, they are called asanas, while Buddhism has its mudras. There are several Tantric and Daoist exercises that are somatic techniques as well.

Qualities of Mind/Heart

Aside from meditation and breathing techniques, spirituality is also about developing certain qualities of the mind and heart. Usually, practitioners look towards developing positive traits, such as detachment, tranquility, loving kindness, equanimity, compassion, truthfulness, and energy. Being mindful, study, and reflecting are also involved in the process.

Chanting

In some paths, chanting can be used for praying, focusing, and studying. When prepping for meditation, chanting can help you focus. In devotional paths, chanting is more about developing getting into surrender and devotion frames of mind. Like someone does when they pray, sometimes practitioners will use chant pieces of text to help them contemplate.

Asceticism

A period of intense self-discipline and simplicity minus self-indulgence is known as asceticism. Some examples of ascetic practices are:

- Fasting
- Abstinence
- Vows of silence
- Meditating for long hours
- Intensive retreats

Think of these like detoxing your mind or cleansing your spirit. Such techniques can help you burn away negative patterns. They also allow you to develop willpower and self-control while proving a sense of contentment. In yoga, such a technique is known as tapas.

Learning, Absorbing, and Understanding

Study or Contemplate

More in tune with the branch of religious spiritualism, this type entails listening to or reading spiritual texts and then contemplating on their meaning deeply. That includes what those texts imply. Followers may read both commentary and foundational literature

– some even memorize what they're reading. When connected with Christianity, this technique is called lectio divina, while it's called swadhyaya in Raja Yoga.

Regardless of the tradition, it's connected to, the study's purpose is to gain insight and understanding. During contemplation, the reader of the texts figures out ways to apply what they've read to their life and change it. The teachings can serve more as models and frameworks that help the readers relate and less as precise descriptions of reality.

Community/Teacher Relationship

A practitioner may enter into a relationship with a teacher or a community of other practitioners. In either case, they can leverage it to learn the tradition and absorb its gist. With the latter, a practitioner will find ready support in case they face difficulties and motivation from learning with like-minded people. The former is a valuable way of finding guidance about the finer aspects of practice.

In some traditions, such personal relationships carry primary importance while the texts are considered secondary. So, a student must form one if they're to continue growing. In others, the transfer of knowledge from student to teacher is via a heart-to-heart transmission. The student spends time with their teacher – called satsang – after being initiated.

Belief

Some spiritual traditions consider faith on the basic tenets as the entry door that leads to their practice. In others, though, belief isn't a requirement, but the experience is. Those include paths like Buddhism and Yoga. To put it another way, the more real progress you experience, the more confident you become in the wisdom behind the tenets of the faith – even those you don't understand yet.

External Action

Ethics

This involves following a set of rules or principles of behavior. For instance, Buddhism has five main precepts:

- Don't harm others
- No lying
- Don't take without permission
- Misbehaving sexually isn't allowed
- Don't use intoxicants

On the surface, these instructions appear very simple, but they actually affect the actions of our bodies, speech, and minds deeply. Most traditions employ this way of truth-seeking.

Ritual

Like rules, a ritual can be a set of actions done for a certain purpose and in the same manner. Followers revere them, take them seriously, and with intensity. Their ultimate aim is not to put up a show but to help followers develop certain feelings or enter a specific state of mind.

Service

Regardless of which kind of community you serve, you're expressing your spiritual commitment with this technique. In addition, you may choose how to perform the said service, such as by:

- Feeding the poor
- Translating scriptures
- Carrying out social reform
- Proving online support to communities

The spiritual aspect of your actions depends on your intention, heart, and attitude instead of the type of work you choose to do.

As the next section will clarify, not every reader needs to do all the training mentioned above. Pick the paths that speak to you best because of their unique flavors.

How to Practice your Beliefs

Everybody has their own spiritual identity. The religion they follow may also add to the way they practice their spirituality. However, a lot of will depend on their personal beliefs. The reverence of some practices, for instance, may seem ordinary to some, while others will have issues with those. Still others will emphasize more on one type of practice than others. Even those people who don't have a religious upbringing may experience spirituality. They may or may not ascribe to a higher power or be a faith-based or religious institution/ community member. In all cases, spirituality is inclusive and fluid. Therefore, it encourages questioning and celebrates the continuity of transformation.

You may be curious about what it takes to develop a spiritual practice. Or, you might be eager to deepen what you already practice. Try doing either in the following ways:

Treat the Body Well

Most importantly, our bodies serve as the home for our mind and spirit. So, if you'd like the latter two to function at optimum levels, your body must be working at peak level too. Does that mean the same to everybody? No! For some, it may involve embracing a diet while it could be something totally different for others. As long as you're doing it in response to what your body's telling you, you're being good to it. After all, your body knows itself best and is practically directing you towards the high-vibe lifestyle perfect for you.

Stop Ignoring your Breath

It's your life source and yet, you're least conscious of your breath! Notice how you breathe when under stress and when you're not. If you're taking short and shallow breaths in stressful situations, change this habit. Full, deep breaths allow more oxygen to flow through the body. They can heal and be life-changing. Those who continue to breathe in the same manner even when not under stress are shallow breathers. Changing it will feel like they're relearning how to breathe!

What does a full deep breath entail? During inhalation, your belly should expand outward while the opposite happens when you exhale. Highly oxygenated blood fuels the organs and nerve cells. It also helps you think more clearly.

Pray and Meditate

It's also possible to cultivate a spiritual practice through prayer and meditation. In addition, these disciplines keep you rooted in the current moment rather than the future or past. Meditation will speak to almost everyone who can practice mindfulness since the two go together. You can use the Headspace app for incredible, affordable and guided sessions. Prayer, on the other hand, would make more sense to you if you subscribe to a higher power.

Go to a Spiritual Retreat

Continue your transformation and spiritual growth by visiting a space that allows for reflection, education, and mentorship. Spiritual retreats can come your way as activities arranged by some institution, or you can opt for a solo getaway. Once you've left your routine and the familiar environment behind, you can recenter yourself more easily. Additionally, you can use them as opportunities for engaging others who are on spiritual paths similar to yours. Learn from them, teach, or learn together!

Get started by checking out this list of spiritual retreats from all over the world. In Europe and Asia, particularly, you'll find many monasteries with setups for self-led retreats and which are inclusive. You'll even discover many that let you pay what and however much you can in exchange! There are many religious and non-religious spiritual retreats within the US, as well. Some even operate on a pay-what-you-can or work exchange system.

Create your Rituals

Think about which of your spiritual rituals is the most meaningful to you. Use it as a beacon and improve on it – or stick to it if it's working well! Whether it's listening to a particular podcast, attending a weekly service, or simply lighting a candle as you contemplate and pray, rituals are meaningful acts that let you practice discipline and reverence. So, pick one that means something in your spiritual practice.

Laugh to Experience Carbonated Holiness

Displaying a little goofiness every now and then can be a transformative spiritual experience. Believers of this discipline consider not taking themselves seriously as a kind of carbonated holiness. Light-heartedness and laughter help us connect to the divine or the most sacred part within ourselves. People who are quick to laugh tend to find success more easily in the Western culture's performance-driven ethos.

Tenderness, too, can be a part of our spiritual practice and connect us with something outside ourselves. So, make time for playful activities that teach you to let go. Engage in the games from your childhood, create art without worrying about it being good or bad, and hold solo dance parties while working in the kitchen.

Spark Forward – 3 Bite-sized Personal Interventions to Improve Matters of the Spirit.

Walking can Double as Meditation

Go on walks often and you won't be confining your spiritual practice to visiting temples or performance of complex rituals! Do it in a purposeful way and be conscious of your surroundings. Let the ambiance clear the mind as you reflect during this brief session of walking meditation. Various religions think walks help people reconnect with themselves.

Give yourself Short Spirit Breaks

Not only will taking regular breaks result in a more relaxed you, it will also improve your work performance, health, and wellness. Instead of scrolling various feeds on your phone during your break, practice calming meditation. Pray without voicing your wishes aloud or do a simple yoga stretch while enjoying the sunshine outside of your office.

Count All Blessings

Sure, it may sound cliched, but counting your blessings can be very a powerful message. Gratitude acts like an antidote to negative emotions. So, maintain a gratitude journal for this simple spiritual practice. Not the journaling kind? Simple reflection will do as well.

Chapter 4 - Conclusion

Everything you'll ever need to know is within you; the secrets of the universe are imprinted on the cells of your body.

Dan Millman

What is Health?

We hope that you enjoyed being on this journey of self-healing with us. Moreover, we're trusting you to realize that it takes more to remain healthy and vibrant than just eating natural, whole foods. That part only nourishes the body. Physical symptoms of mental stress, such as patches of eczema and headaches, will show that you can follow healthy diets all you want. But if you don't connect them with the aspect that is in need of help, you won't get rid of said symptoms.

Some other symptoms of stress that might show up include:

- Fatigue
- Upset stomach
- Muscle pain
- Sleep issues

When stress affects you on a physical level, one or more of these indications will show up. Like a stubborn patch of eczema somewhere on your body. Anything you do, including eliminating foods one by one to check for the culprit, have no effect on it. So, you'll need to consider the other two fundamental aspects of your beings for reasons. When the three components, body, mind, and spirit, work in tandem, they create a state of radiant health.

Interesting enough, each one is quite different from the other two. For instance, the body is physical and organic. It carries us around in the physical world and is the channel for our interaction within it. On the other hand, the mind manifests as personality, emotions, thoughts, and interactions. Your body shapes your mind's interpretations, as does the physical world. Then, there's the subconscious effect that your spirit has on the mind. In a way, the mind is the communication and reception center for your body and soul. They are inseparably linked together, which means that they must work in harmony if you want to remain healthy.

You may call your soul creative energy that connects to the universe. It transcends spiritual beliefs and can give you a sense of fulfillment and joy with life – provided you can find where's it hidden deep within. Letting your creativity run wild and doing what you love nourishes the soul.

In conclusion, all three aspects are connected to each other.

What should the reader do now?

The first things to usually come to mind when we think about our health are diet and exercise. However, as mentioned before, good health is about more than the physical body. We'd also have to factor in the wellness of our mind and spirit. Emotional wellbeing, for instance, is crucial for our betterment. If a stressful situation causes us to think negatively, we may manifest physical pain or illness as the symptoms.

So, we shortlisted the many things you can do in your daily life for overall wellness. Then, we simplified them into a smaller list of 12 ways that result in the cultivation of mind-body-soul balance.

Here they are:

1. **Become a reader and learner.** You shouldn't stop yourself from learning once you complete your schooling. Education does more than just get you a good job; it can open your mind to new beliefs, possibilities, and interests. Keep that going for yourself by reading, attending workshops, taking online classes, and watching documentaries.

2. **Meditate regularly.** The advantages you'll enjoy, courtesy of daily meditation sessions, are so many. They include improvements in memory, creativity, attention, sleep, mood, and immune system function. And you enjoy all of those benefits by just spending a few minutes spent in meditation every day! Since guided meditation is more suitable for beginners, we suggest you start with this 30-Day Meditation Challenge.

3. **Do yoga.** It's amazing for your health since it will help the body build strength and coordination and make it more flexible. In addition, it calms your mind and lets you tap into the mind-body-soul connection.

4. **Avoid sitting down for extended periods.** Even those who have a job that binds them to a desk should attempt to move around. Too much sitting down leaves you open to the risks of heart disease and diabetes. It may also shorten a lifespan.

5. **Get a moderate to fast-paced workout going each day.** Even if you're doing it for just 15 minutes or take as long as it takes you to walk to your office nearby, do it! Exercise keeps the heart healthy, improves mood, and is crucial for building physical stamina.

6. **Go outside more.** Take part in any of the various nature-based activities, such as fruit picking, foraging for wild foods, hiking, outdoor sports, boating, camping, and picnics.

7. **Eat more plant-based foods.** Veggies and fruits can prevent chronic disease. When shopping for them, do so at the local farmer's market. That way, you will find organic, fresh, and in-season produce.

8. **Fuel those passions.** Indulge in things that make your soul happy, such as swimming, painting, gardening, dancing, writing, and making music. In short, anything that doesn't feel like work or a chore but brings you genuine joy can be on your list of passions!

9. **Be grateful.** Write about the things and people that you're grateful for. Do it as often as you can if daily journaling isn't possible.

10. **Be kind.** To everyone and yourself!

11. **Never compromise on sleep.** Get as much of it as needed daily, and don't think naps won't do you as much good as they did back in kindergarten.

12. **Go natural.** Throw out as many synthetic products and opt for natural, including those you use on yourself for skincare or your home.

So, which of these steps are you excited to try out? Which of these do you already do?

Words of Inspiration

All three aspects of you are connected, so they form a cycle. Each component of that cycle influences and is influenced by the others. Thus, if they are not in harmony with each other, you'd experience a cycle of disease as opposed to a cycle of health if they are.

The soul is at the center of that cycle since it is the essence of our being and represents our true self. Follow your passions and keep doing what you love doing to feed the soul. Believe it or not, when you express your creativity, you follow your path and know joy, peace, and fulfillment.

Consequently, the satiated soul exerts a positive effect on the mind. The latter expresses that effect in terms of positive emotions and thoughts. It also manifests in the positive relations you have with others. So, keep expressing kindness and love towards yourself and others.

The next stage of the cycle is all about the body. A physical manifestation that reflects the positivity of your mind and soul. If you're loving towards it, it means you'll take care of your body by eating healthy and engaging in regular exercise.

A version of you that's physically well and energized would have the motivation to continue doing the things you enjoy – and thus, feeding the soul. Think of this cycle as self-perpetuating and result in a wholesome you!

Chapter 5 - Moving Forward

Health is an announcement of agreement between your body, mind and spirit. Honor your body, keep it in good shape. When you are not healthy, look to see which parts of you disagree. Your body will demonstrate the truth to you. Notice what it is showing you, listen to what it is saying.

Neale Donald Walsch

To continue learning about the three aspects that make you whole, for product references to help with your journey, motivation, and getting updates, view my website www.sparklifechange.com.

Acknowledgment

For Dad

This book is written in the loving memory of my father, who we lost way too early.

You are truly missed each and every day.

For Mom

Your love and support is unwavering. Thank you for your teacher skills that helped make this book what it is today. Thank you and I love you!

For My Wife

For I will always be your Sudafed, and you will forever be the love of my life.

All characters in this book have no existence outside the author's imagination and have no relation whatsoever to anyone's name or names. They are not inspired by anyone known or unknown to the author, and all incidents are based on the author's imagination.

www.ingramcontent.com/pod-product-compliance
Lightning Source LLC
LaVergne TN
LVHW052044160826
845678LV00015B/3113

9798535711539